AN EMOTION
OF HEART

JITESH KUMAR

ISBN 979-888555692-7

we always dedicate our attainment to the one who has been the reason behind it.

someone who came in my life and ran alone in the twinkling of an eye. That someone was "My first love" and this first love has given me the reason to pick the pen up and write the pain down. She has become the source of my emotions. Emotion comes from her, belongs to her and goes to her.

she is now like a moon for me, exists but inaccessible. But where ever she is now will always live in my heart. Today this book has been written by me just because of her, it's just like she is ink and i am the pen, lives in me but can not be touched by me. Finally i want to dedicate this book to her and want to thank her to be in my life and made me to feel the love.

Contents

Contents

Contents

Contents

About Poetic Souls

Poetic Souls is writers community, where we grow together while helping each other.

Motivation and ideas is what we all seek and give.

Prompts, Challenges and various activities help a writer to think beyond the box and helps in their overall development.

Apart from this we also provide an author platform which encourages budding writer's to enhance their skills and make their work, reach a target audience of potential readers. ...

Its a growing community of the writers, managed by Rohan Nath and Nidhi Shukla.

Preface

Poetry is a form of literature that uses aesthetic and often rhythmic qualities of language – such as phonaesthetics, sound symbolism, and metre – to evoke meanings in addition to, or in place of, a prosaic ostensible meaning. Poetry has a long and varied history, evolving differentially across the globe.

poetry- less words and much emotions. This book is written to convey an emotion of an author Jitesh kumar beautifully, it paints a picture of what the poet feels about the thing, person, idea, concept or even an object. The main motive and the soul purpose of this book is to heal the wounded hearts. people who suffer with their pain in alone and those who couldn't talk to self, this book will make them to feel inside of an individual so one can heal the pain. Reading or writing poetry creates a space for empathy, for seeing another person, for bearing witness to our common humanity. Whether it's written or spoken, poetry can be a powerful tool to aid in healing. It offers an opportunity for readers, writers, and speakers to feel both heard and understood. Here's a reminder that our very humanity rests on the compassion we show each other. It's half poem, half prayer.

It's all praise for a world made better by the way we love each other, and by the way we love ourselves. The poet Jitesh is inspired by his own life full of wax and wane, he started writing two years back and this book contains the poems based on his real life experiences. He wants to enumerate the pain of every individual and take it inside him so he can write more beautifully and deeply and with this he

will heal everyone's pain as well. we hope that these handful
of poems are able to
bring a bright smile on your lovely faces.
With this, we feel immense pleasure to present
before you all.
Happy Reading loved ones!
How do you like these poems ? Don't forget to ping me up to
share your experience.
I promise, I will read every single one, and I'd love to know
what you think.

Acknowledgements

*First and foremost i would like to say that i am deeply grateful
to God almighty
For being able to publish my first debut and solo book "An
Emotion Of Heart"
In the insubstantial time structure.
Furthermore i would like to thank and express my
gratitude to Poetic Souls
Publication for providing me this significant opportunity
to publish my first
Book for what i am waiting for since a long.
As every writer wants to have a book of his name in the
whole world's hands
And Poetic Souls Publication is making my dream
accomplished by giving a golden chance to showcase my talent
to this whole world,
with this i can be a voice of immumerable voicesless
people out there.
So A Very Big Thank You to Poetic Souls Publication.
Next, i would like to thank my Parents, both of my mom
and dad
"Mrs. Usha Devi and Mr. Brajesh Kumar" have supported
and stood with
me throughout the time, in all the bad and dark days i
have faced.
I could never be able to walk ahead with all this without
them, i will always
be indebted to them.
Furthermore, my brothers, cousins and all of my friends
who always supports*

me to keep my work on, guides me and always motivates me whenever i feel low. Some of relatives, friends and followers who have been appreciating me for my work that boosted my confidence and encouraged me a lot that leads me to publish my book.

A very big thank you to every one of them.

Last but not least, to all my dear readers, thank you so much for your love and support. This one is just for you.

I would like to dedicate this book to all the readers and to each and every person who felt the love once, who love someone, who know how life goes being in love. Being in relationship needs both of two sides but being in love just needs you, so if you have come on this planet just live the life filled with love and spread the love.

In this world, where people have many different platforms like gadgets, social media and cinema to enjoy, it's rare to find a classic person like you who buys a book and sits back patiently and reading it like listening the words and making a scence in mind and watching it as well.

So here's to every single person who spent a few bucks to buy this book,

you deserve a big "Thank You",

i love you all.

Prologue

This book named "An Emotion Of Heart" which is written by Jitesh Kumar, also known as Jikku, has put his pain and all the emotions into the blank papers in the form of words. These words have taken a shape of poems and quotes and in this book you will be going through those poems and quotes which has been shown also with the painting and sketches scenery.

Jitesh has written these poems from his own life episodes, from all the peaks and valleys and from the moment of heart breaks, loneliness and depression.

But this is not all, Jitesh has mentioned even about his love, how beautiful she looks and shines and the life he had with her and the life he wanted to be with her in future, how much he loved and loves her, from how long he is waiting for her and the way he wants to love her when he will meet her again and this book is asking her loudly when you will be back again.

Jitesh wants each of you to fill the words inside the heart and utter it when you sit alone to talk to yourself. Words have power that we will be enchanted by this.

The influence of words on us is magical and beautiful.

Jitesh tried his best to do the same for all of you and even to write with the simple and sober words so each and every can understand and feel this.

He has started writing these poems in the end of 2019 when he lost his love, after that he started sitting before sunset where he used to sit with her and writing all his real life moments what he did and what he couldn't. The moment when he met her for the last time and even didn't know this was his meeting with her, he always thinks if he could know

about it, he could hug her for some more time and what if he could meet one more time knowing it's his last meeting so he can say everything to her, complete his every moment with her and in the end he can mark a full stop on it, what if ?
This book is all about heart and emotions or nothing else so Jitesh has named it "An Emotion Of Heart" but these are many emotions and Jitesh thinks thousands of emotions are even an "Emotion" and he wants from all of you to feel it.

About The Author

Jitesh kumar, also known as Jikku, is a vigorous writer from kota,
India. He is very passionate about writing and he aims to
be productive with his passion and career.
Recently he has completed his bachelor's degree in
computer science engineering and now he is working as a
Graphic Designer.
He is 22 years old, trying to express him in front of this world and
he knows that this world needs to be loved more. His
poetry is all about to live a life full of love.
It has been two years now when he started writing because of
an incident when he lost his love, he picked the pen and tried
to put all his pain on a blank paper and now all that led
him here.
He says that he can't write a single word when his heart is silent
but when it says even a single word he can write a page on it.
This Book is his solo and debut book. A man who has big
dreams in life, has started going on it's path.
He believes in God (Lord Krishna) and try to walk on krishna's path,
He have read Shrimad Bhagawad Gita and he asks people to read it
and act upon it because no question is there whose answer is not given in it.

Next to God, his family is entire world to him and he aims to accomplish every dream of his parents. At the age of nine, he lost his uncle, was just 24, in an accident. He was greatly
pampered by his uncle and loosing him was the biggest holocaust
for him.
Either writing or any art comes from heart, heart which has pain and he believes that every single person have the same pain with different stories so he writes the way people can relate and somewhere these words can heal their pain. it's impossible to meet every single person and hug them so he wants to hug this world by his words. And he believes these words can be voice of voiceless people around the world.
He believes in self and wants to bring something that motivates and inspire his surrounding people by which they start believing in themselves too because acoording to him we are all upto so much more than we can ever imagine.
His verse
"that's the way of life,
everything that happened is right"
contains a positive spirit that everything happens, happens for a reason and for a better tomorrow. He felt down when he lost his love but he couldn't be able to write if that would't be happened.
Jikku loves watching cricket and cheering for india. He is inspired by
Indian writer Javed Akhtar sahab and Gulzar sahab, he loves reading them. Jikku wants to be a business man along with an author and poet. He has interest in journalism, he wants to study further in journalism and change the way of representing it.

ABOUT THE AUTHOR

*He wants to save this world from shattering and bring peace
to mankind, he believes that his efforts will help
wounding up the readers.
And with this,
Jikku has written this book which is his first ever project
in which
He has put his whole heart and soul.*

CHAPTER ONE

Quotes

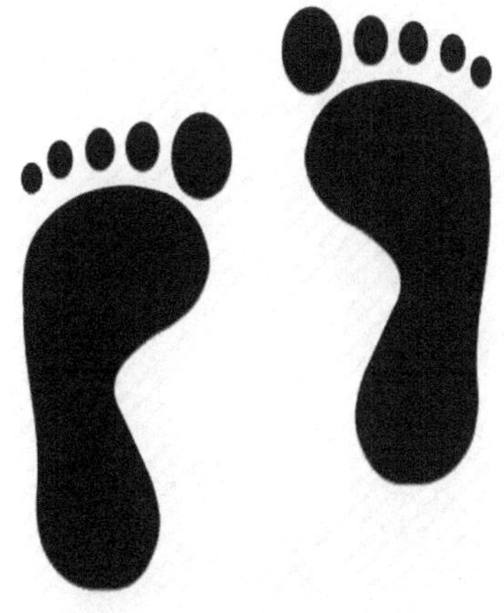

*MILLIONS OF RAIN DROPS CAN'T EVEN ERASE THE
MARKS
OF YOUR FEET FROM HERE,
WHICH WERE PRINTED WHEN
YOU CAME RUNNING TO HUG ME.
I AM WALKING ON THE SAME PATH TO REACH
YOU,
WISH I COULD YOU AGAIN.*

Quotes

"CAN I HUG YOU?"
DOES'T ALWAYS MEAN HE WANTS TO HUG,
SOMETIMES IT MEANS HE WANTS TO BE HUGGED.

CHAPTER THREE

Quotes

VIRGINITY DOESN'T DECIDE SANCTITY.

Quotes

CHAIN STOPPED
CLOUDS ARE CLEARED
SITTING ON THE TERRACE

JITESH KUMAR

COLD WIND HITTING THE FACE
HOLDING A CUP OF TEA
PHONE ASIDE
EARPHONES PLUGGED IN
YOU ARE ON CALL
SEE, MY WORLD IS SO SMALL.

Quotes

*WHEN YOU MISS SOMETHING TO DO IN NIGHT
THEN YOU AUTOMATICALLY GET UP EARLY IN
THE MORNING,
I AM FINDING THAT SOMETHING TO MISS EVERY
NIGHT.*

BASED ON TITANIC MOVIE SCENE

AND I SAID TO GOD, TAKE IT LIKE MY LAST WISH
BUT I WANT TO PERCEIVE THE BELLE OF THE OCEAN
AND IN THAT MOMENT I MET YOU, YOU WERE JUST
LOOKING LIKE THAT BELLE OF THE OCEAN
AND THAT DEITY GRANTED ME TO STAY IN THAT
OCEAN TO FEEL IT

FOR REST OF MY LIFE.
WORLD ! I WAS NOT DYING,
SOMEBODY WAS CONSUMMATING THAT LAST
WISH.

Quotes

THIS COLD WIND OF MIDNIGHT EVOKES FROM HER BODY AND SAYS AS THE SAME WAY AS YOUR BODY EVOKES AND SAYS TO ME, "I WANT YOU TO FEEL ME."

Quotes

THE RUSTLING WIND OF AUTUMN DAYS
RUBBING ON MY FACE
REMINDS ME YOUR ANKLET CHIME
WHEN YOU DANCED WITH ME
FOR THE FIRST TIME.

Quotes

WILL BE TOGETHER, LET'S HOPE
WILL BE IN ARMS, TOO CLOSE
WILL TOUCH YOUR SOUL, A LIVE SHOW
WILL GIVE YOU A RIDE, A RUNNING HORSE
UNDER THE SHINING STARS, LIGHTS OFF.

Quotes

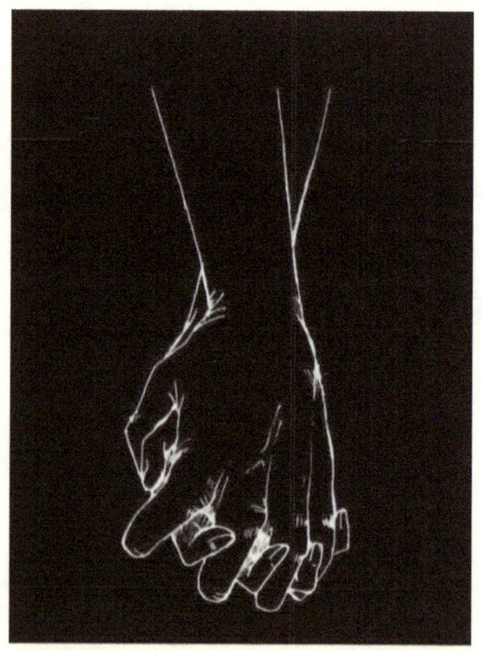

Don't know what is left behind in the first love.
Whomever you see, remembers the same.

Quotes

I am black as leaf,
She is milky white
Where else you can get better tea than this ?

Quotes

She is the moon in night
And ocean in the light,
I watched her until she disappeared
She gifted me to swim inside.

CHAPTER THIRTEEN

Quotes

YOU ARE THE STAR THAT I WANT YOU TO FALL DOWN IN MY LAP AND IN THE SAME MOMENT MY WISH GETS COMPLETED.

Quotes

YOU ARE THE PAIN
AND I AM THE TEARS,
YOU CAN BE WITHOUT ME
I CAN'T BE WITHOUT YOU.

Quotes

AND I AM WATCHING THE BRIGHT STARS IN THE
DARK SPACE BETWEEN THE TWO BEAUTIFUL
CURVES,
YEAH ! TONIGHT, SHE IS SLEEPING NAKED UNDER
THE MOON.

Quotes

How can I forget you?
If i couldn't be of this night,
then should I stop sleeping?

Quotes

THE INBOX BECOMES A WARM BED,
WHENEVER WE TALK TILL THE BRIGHT.

Quotes

*Even you can't control yourself to fall in love with the one who
is already committed.*

Quotes

HOLDING YOUR WAIST THE WAY I HOLD MY CUP OF TEA,
KISSING YOUR LIPS LIKE IT'S A HONEYCOMB AND I AM THE BEE.

Quotes

ONCE AGAIN I HAVE BEEN FILLED WITH LOVE, COME BACK ! I WANNA RELEASE IT IN YOU.

Quotes

THE REGRET IS THAT WE COULDN'T SAY OUR
KIND OF GOOD BYE TO EACH OTHER.

Travel Again

I WANT TO TRAVEL AGAIN,
WITH THE SAME ROADS, WITH THE SAME SONGS
WITH THE SAME WEATHER, WITH THE SAME
SWEATER
I KNOW THIS TIME YOU WON'T BE THERE FOR ME

BUT THESE ALL SMELL LIKE YOU.
I WANT TO TRAVEL AGAIN TO SMELL YOU.....

Quotes

I WISH JUST FOR THE ONE LAST TIME
WE COULD MEET.

CHAPTER TWENTY-FOUR

Quotes

DENY BUT DON'T IGNORE
REJECTION MAKES ONE TO IMPROVE HIMSELF
WHEREAS IGNORANCE MAKES ONE TO SMASH
THE OTHERSELF.

Quotes

DON'T KNOW WHY YOU FEEL LIKE MY LAST SIP OF TEA

*BECAUSE AFTER THAT THERE WAS NOTHING
LEFT TO ENJOY.*

Quotes

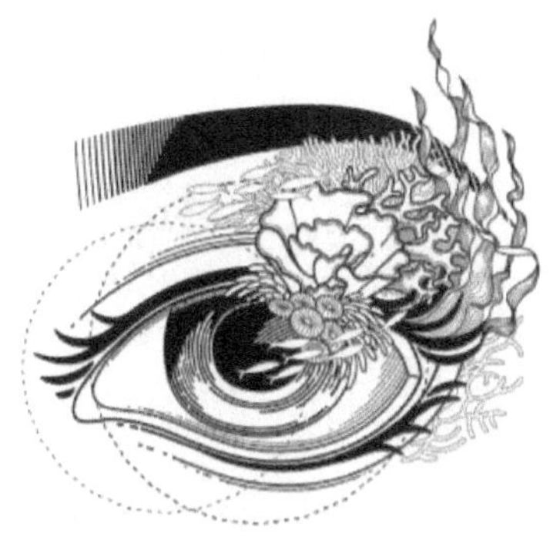

THE LAST YOU SAID
" SEE YOU LATER",
AND NOW YOU HAVE BECOME MOONWATER.

Quotes

YOUR BIRTH DATE GIVES ME THE VOYAGE
WHERE THE OCEAN CONSISTS MY TEARS
AND SPACE YOUR EMPTINESS.

Moon Gives Smile

*WE ARE EAGER TO ATTAIN FOR WHAT ONE
CRAVES
THIS IS DELUSIONAL DOING TWO BRAVES
MAKING YOU SLEEP TWHERE THE PILLOW IS MY
THIGHS*

RUBBING YOUR CHEEKS AND THERE MOON GIVES SMILES.

Quotes

FROM THE MOON LIGHT,
I AM TALKING TO YOUR SLOW BREATHES SO I CAN
WATCH THIS CUTE LITTLE SLEEPING FACE GETTING
ILLUMINATED BY THE FIRST RAY OF SUN LIGHT.

Memories

YOUR MEMORY HITS DIFFERENT SOMEDAY
AS THE SAME SONG HITS DIFFERENT SOMEDAY
FEET ARE TAKING A SCARY STEP
SOMEONE OVER THERE PULLING ME BACK

PULLING ME TO THE TIME WHEN YOU SAID
THERE IS A COMPLETE LIFE AHEAD
SO DON'T WORRY WILL FIND A WAY
WE WILL MEET DIFFERENT SOMEDAY.

Quotes

I WISH WHEN WE LAST MEET
I COULD HUG YOU MORE UNDER THAT FLYOVER,
AND LET THEM ALL WAIT
THE MOON THE SON AND THAT CAB DRIVER.

Quotes

*THE MOMENT YOU PERCEIVE THERE IS NO ONE
ELSE
WHO CAN LOVE YOUR PARTNER MORE THAN YOU
YOU START LIVING THEIR SOUL TOO.*

Quotes

BRING HER IN PRESENT

OR PULL ME REVERSE
WHERE I WAS THE ROCKET
AND SHE WAS THE UNIVERSE

COMING TO THINK OF "THAT HUG"

*COMING TO THINK OF "THAT HUG" :
WHEN OUR BODIES GRABBED US HERE IN THE
SAME BEAUTIFUL EVENING AND MADE OUR
SHADOWS ONE
AND WE BOTH WERE FINDING EACH OTHER IN
THAT SHADOW AND
YOU TOLD ME THAT I CAN'T LEAVE YOU UNTIL I
FIND MYSELF IN THAT
SHADOW AND THE BEST PART WAS EVEN I
COULDN'T.*

Quotes

SOME PEOPLE JUST FALL INTO HEART
BY THEIR TALKS AND LITTLE CUTE ACTS
AND I THINK THAT IS MUCH BETTER

THAN ANY OUTER BEAUTY.

Quotes

*IN THE DARKEST ROOM WHEN THE ELECTRONS
IN MY BLOOD
GET INCREASED, BY YOUR FOUR FINGERS THE
BODY PAIN WILL BE DECREASED AND IN THAT
MOMENT WHEN THE ENTIRE WORLD WILL SLEEP
AND I WILL TAKE YOU TO THE UNIVERSE OF RELIEF
THERE YOU WILL MEET THE SOUND WHICH CALLED*

AN EMOTION OF HEART

PEACE.

CHAPTER THIRTY-SEVEN

Quotes

*YOU CAN'T GRAB THE TIME BUT YOU CAN GRAB
THE MOMENT
MOMENT WHICH BRINGS A SMILE ON YOUR FACE.*

Quotes

*WHY YOU LOVE SUNSET A LOT
WHEN YOU ARE HAVING YOUR MOON.*

Quotes

*WHEN IT'S ABOUT LOVE THE BODY BECOMES
TRANSPARENT
SO THE PAIN CAN DIRECTLY HIT THE SOUL AND
THRASH IT.*

CHAPTER FORTY

Quotes

I WILL LOVE YOU...THE DAY I WILL BE ALL MINE.

Quotes

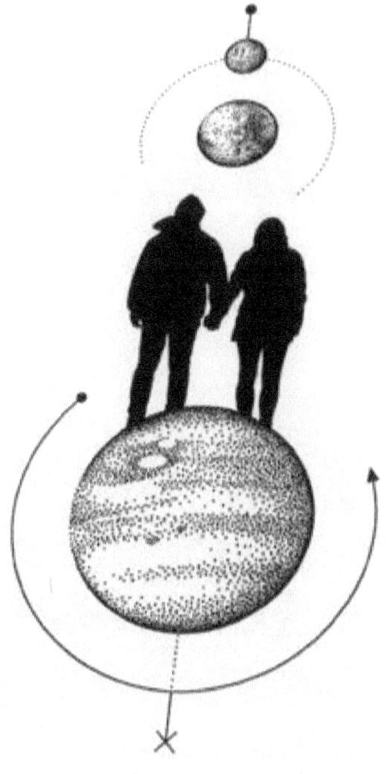

TWO SIDES OF MY COIN,
WAIT FOR HER OR FORGET HER
BUT NEVER HAVE THE COURAGE TO TOSS.

Quotes

YOUR PARENTS ARE THE ONLY EXCEPTIONS
OF YOUR CONTACT LIST WHO CAN TALK TO
YOU WHENEVER YOU NEED.

Quotes

SHE BROKE THAT MIRROR VERY CRUELLY
IN WHICH SHE USED TOO SEE HERSELF
EVERYDAY.

Coldest Moon

HE : AND I GUESS ONLY IN YOUR ARMS...RIGHT?
"YOU ARE THE COLDEST MOON I AM HOLDING
TONIGHT,
AND GIVING ME THE WARM LIKE I AM SITTING
BEFORE A LIGHT (SUN),
AS FIRST TIME I AM LIVING A COMPLETE DAY, A
COMPLETE NIGHT,

I AM LOOKING INTO YOURS JUST LOOK INTO
MINE,
TILL THEN LET'S MAKE A SIGHT
LIKE WHERE OUR LIPS CAN DO FIGHT,
AND I GUESS ONLY...
SHE : RIGHT !

Quotes

AN EMOTION OF HEART

*EVEN IF YOU LEAVE ME THE SAME WAY IN THE
NEXT LIFE,
THIS HEART STILL WANTS TO MEET YOU ONLY.*

CHAPTER FORTY-SIX

Quotes

*LITERALLY IT'S MOST DIFFICULT THING IN THE
WORLD
TO MAKE PEOPLE LAUGH BUT THE BEST PART IS,
WE CAN TRY
AND IF WE GET SUCCEED
BELIEVE ME IT'S MOST BEAUTIFUL THING IN THE
WORLD.*

CHAPTER FORTY-SEVEN

Quotes

AND IN THAT SOMETIME,
COUNTING YOUR LOVE,
DID YOU LOVE ME EVER,
OR IT ALL WAS A SYMPATHY IN THE NAME OF
CARE,
WHY EVERYTIME I GOT KILLED AND BE THE
SAVER,
WELL, CAN YOU GIVE ME A FAVOUR?
LET'S LEAVE FOR FOREVER.

Quotes

*HOPEFULLY I TURNED BACK BUT NO EYES WERE
LOOKING AT ME,
I FOUND ME ALONE AGAIN.*

limitless Thirst

*YOU JUST CAME FOR A MOMENT AND NO LIMIT WAS
THERE OF MY JOY,
THEN JUST WENT AWAY AND NO SCALE WAS
THERE TO MEASURE MY CRY,
AT LEAST YOU COULD ASK ABOUT THE
CONDITION OF MY HEART,
YOU ARE LIKE WATER WHERE I AM LIKE THIRSTY
DESERT
NOTHING I DID SUCH TO MAKE YOU ANNOYED
I THINK NOW THE GENERATION OF LOVE HAS
BEEN DESTRYOED.*

Quotes

MANY OF MY FRIENDS ONCE SAID TO ME
"I AM BUSY, TALK TO YOU LATER",
WHO HAVEN'T COME YET.

CHAPTER FIFTY-ONE

Sinking in Love

HE WAS SINKING IN THE OCEAN OF LOVE,
SO MANY BOATS OVER THERE WERE WATCHING
HIM CONSIDERING
THAT HE IS SWIMMING IN IT AND ENJOYING,
BUT HE WAS SCREAMING LOUDER UNDER THE
OCEAN AS HE COULD,
ASKING FOR A SINGLE HAND WHO CAN PULL HIM
UP AND SAVE,
BUT NO HANDS CAME TO HIM.

*THE ONE WHO WAS ALIVE, TODAY IS NOT.
NOW THE DEATH BODY IS SWIMMING AND
ENJOYING, AND NOW THE SAME BOATS ARE GIVING
THEIR HANDS TO PULL HIM UP, CONSIDERING HE IS
SINKING.*

CHAPTER FIFTY-TWO

I Wish

*I WISH THAT YOU COULD BE
MY NEIGHBOUR, MY COLLEGEMATE, MY FRIEND'S
FRIEND
OR AT LEAST FROM THE SAME CITY,
SO EVEN AFTER GETTING SEPARATED I COULD
SEE YOU
WALKING, TALKING, SMILING
AND THE LOUDER SILENCE ON YOUR CUTE FACE.
I WISH YOU COULD BE...*

CHAPTER FIFTY-THREE

My Satisfactions

WHENEVER I WRITE SOMETHING ABOUT HER
I ALWAYS SEND THAT IN THE SAME INBOX
WHERE WE USED TO TALK,
YA I KNOW I AM IN HER BLOCKLIST NOW,
SHE CAN'T MAKE IT SEEN BUT I ALWAYS GET A
INNER SATISFACTION
THAT IT'S GONE FROM MY SIDE.

Quotes

FROM

GETTING SMILE LOOKING AT THE PICTURE
TO
GETTING TEARS LOOKING AT THE SAME PICTURE
A JOURNEY HAS ENDED.

CHAPTER FIFTY-FIVE

Quotes

In this way everyone has shadow in the light.
If you can be in the dark too, then tell me.

Quotes

A SHIRT, I LOVE BUT DON'T WEAR
A SONG, I LOVE BUT DON'T LISTEN
A WEATHER, I LOVE BUT DON'T FEEL
A PLACE, I LOVE BUT DON'T VISIT
JUST BECAUSE OF YOU.

Quotes

A UNIQUE IMAGE OF SIMPLICITY,
WHY NOT TO DECORATE HER WITH FLOWERS
TONIGHT,
TONIGHT, TWO BODIES WILL BE SCORCHED ON
THE BED,
SO IN THE EVENING, LET'S GET THE LOVE
EXTEMELY WET.

Quotes

THE SHARPNESS OF YOUR MEMORIES WILL SCRAP
THE SHEATH
OF MY COTTON'S HEART.

Quotes

TAKE ME TO SOMEWHERE IN THE OPEN SKY,

AN EMOTION OF HEART

AND LEAVE.

CHAPTER SIXTY

HER FINGER ON MY LIPS,
WE WERE CLOSER TO THE KISS,
SHE BENT DOWN ON MY FACE,
JUST REMOVED THE SPACE,
FOUR EYES WERE CLOSED,
FOUR LIPS WERE LOCKED,
AND WE KISSED TILL THE BRIGHT.

CHAPTER SIXTY-ONE

Quotes

*WANT TO MEET HER AGAIN FOR THE ONE LAST
TIME,
JUST TO FORGET HER.*

CHAPTER SIXTY-TWO

Quotes

*THE DAY I MET HER FOR THE FIRST TIME IT WAS HER
BIRTHDAY
AND I DIDN'T KNOW ABOUT THAT SO I COULDN'T
WISH HER BUT I HAD HER IN MY LIFE...
AFTER YEARS ON THE SAME DAY I KNOW IT'S HER
BIRTHDAY BUT NOW I DON'T HAVE HER TO WISH.*

CHAPTER SIXTY-THREE

Quotes

CAN EAT BY ANY HANDS,
JUST MORSEL MUST BE OF LOVE.

Quotes

EGO IS ALL ABOUT,
"HOW YOU FINISHED YOUR LAST CONVERSATION"

CHAPTER SIXTY-FIVE

Quotes

For Not to bring back those days
Come only to narrate the tales of those days!

Quotes

Then some other day I will write about her beauty,
Let me just take a look today.

Quotes

Today love has just become fascinated by the body
Like the past has taken away everyone's soul.

Quotes

*"Love makes me cry all day,
Then the evening reminds me of home"
my daily routine.*

CHAPTER SIXTY-NINE

Quotes

How close you both are ?
Where two drops of sweat collide and be the one.

Quotes

I LOVED, I LOVE AND I'LL LOVE
ONLY
THE ONE,THE ONE, THE ONE
WHO
WASN'T, ISN'T AND WON'T
WITH ME,WITH ME,WITH ME.

Quotes

- Hey ! Tree , sky and moon
please tell me "She is coming soon".

Quotes

These streets of my city are twinkling the way you give smiles,
Some like your lips, some like your eyes,
Some like your waist and some like your thighs.

Quotes

the warm bed, warm you
grabbing the cold me,
tonight I will be a puck
please don't scold me,
the soft bed, soft you
rubbing the bold me,

AN EMOTION OF HEART

tonight let it stuck
let me be my old me.

Quotes

Climbing the highest mountain of this planet,
"The dream of getting you seems like the same."

Destiny Is With You

The sky is with you,
With you the clouds are,
the ocean is with you,
with you the drops are,
the night is with you,
with you the dreams are,
the moon is the with you,
with you the stars are,
the music is with you,
with you the songs are,
the garden is with you,
with you the flowers are,
the love is with you,
with you the struggles are,
the destination is with you,
with you the paths are.

www.ingramcontent.com/pod-product-compliance
Lightning Source LLC
Chambersburg PA
CBHW031339160726
47993CB00002B/753